Re
Book
& Guidance

For use with the following lettings:

England

- Assured and Assured Periodic Tenancies
- Restricted Contract Lettings
- Protected or Statutory Tenancies
- Lodgers (including Wales)

Scotland

- Assured and Short Assured Tenancies
- Lodgers

Northern Ireland

- Private Tenancies
- Lodgers

DOWNLOADS

Purchase of this Rent Book entitles you to free downloads.

For more information and access to downloads, go to:

www.lawpack.co.uk/f005

Enter registration code:

F0051108841

when asked

EXCLUSION OF LIABILITY AND DISCLAIMER

Whilst every effort has been made to ensure that this Lawpack product provides accurate and expert guidance, it is impossible to predict all the circumstances in which it may be used. Accordingly, neither the publisher, authors, nor any barristers or solicitors who have assisted in the production of this Lawpack product and updated or refined it, or whose name is credited as having so assisted and updated or refined it, nor retailers, nor any other suppliers shall be liable to any person or entity with respect to any loss or damage caused or alleged to be caused as a result of the use of the information contained in or omitted from this Lawpack product.

Lawpack Publishing gives you a limited guarantee. If for any reason you are not happy with your purchase, you may return this Lawpack product to us with your receipt within 30 days of the date of purchase for a full refund. In no event shall our liability exceed the purchase price of this Lawpack product. Use of this Lawpack product constitutes acceptance of these terms.

About Rent Books

This Rent Book and Guidance provides instructions for collecting and recording the payment of rent in any of the following letting situations:

- Assured and Assured Periodic Tenancies in England
- Restricted Contract Lettings in England
- Protected or Statutory Tenancies in England
- Assured and Short Assured Tenancies in Scotland
- Private Tenancies in Northern Ireland
- Lodgers in England, Wales, Scotland and Northern Ireland

Rent is the money which a tenant pays the landlord in exchange for their right to occupy the property.

In **England and Northern Ireland** the payment of rent is not absolutely required in order to create a tenancy, but in Scotland it is vital.

In **England and Scotland** a rent book is only required:

- where the rent is described in the tenancy agreement as being paid weekly; or
- where the rent is actually paid weekly by agreement, irrespective of the wording of the agreement.

Where rent is being demanded or paid weekly, it is a criminal offence to fail to provide a rent book.

Where a rent book is required to be provided it is also an obligation that it is kept reasonably up to date. The purpose of a rent book is to provide a receipt for payments for the tenant and a log of rent paid for the landlord. Therefore, it is useless to have such a book and then allow it to become hopelessly outdated.

Rent is payable in arrears, unless the tenancy agreement states otherwise, and most modern agreements do. In the case of tenancies in England which fall under the Rent Act 1977 ('statutory tenants'), it is unlawful to demand rent in advance and all of these tenancies will have the rent paid in arrears. Where payment is due, it falls due on the morning of the day stated in the agreement but the tenant has the whole of that day (until midnight) to make payment. Where rent is payable in advance, the tenant will be deemed to be in arrears for the whole period that they are obliged to make payment for once that payment is outstanding. So, if a tenant is supposed to make a payment on the first day of each month in advance for the coming month, the tenant will be one month in arrears if he does not make payment on that day.

Where rent is payable in advance there is no requirement in law that the payment be apportioned and this is only required if the tenancy agreement allows for it. So, if a tenant makes advance payment for a full month and then departs the property part way through the month (even if they do so with the landlord's agreement) then the landlord is under no obligation to refund the money for the unused portion of that month (even if they relet the property), unless they have specifically agreed to do so.

In **Northern Ireland**, the provision of a rent book is compulsory for all tenancies and the landlord commits a criminal offence if he fails to do so. The offence is committed every time the rent is demanded and every 14 days during the tenancy in any event, so a landlord who does not provide a rent book can find themselves being prosecuted for multiple counts of failing to provide the document. Each offence currently has a maximum fine of £2,500.

For **lodgers**, the money paid is, legally speaking, not rent but simply a 'licence fee', as lodgers do not have tenancies. Homeowners should be careful not to describe money paid as 'rent' if they are not creating a tenancy, as it causes confusion and may give the occupier more rights than they intend. However, you cannot avoid creating a tenancy by falsely describing a rent payment as something else. The provision of this book to a non-tenant will not in itself be enough to allow the tenant to assert that they are paying money as rent, despite its title.

The tenant/lodger should read the information beginning on page 3.

The landlord should fill in the table below.

TENANCY/LODGER DETAILS (LANDLORD TO COMPLETE)
TENANT/LODGER:
DATE OF TENANCY/LODGER AGREEMENT:
RENT COLLECTOR:
PROPERTY ADDRESS:

TYPE OF LETTING (LANDLORD MUST TICK APPLICABLE BOX)		
A		**ASSURED TENANCY** (ENGLAND)
B		**ASSURED PERIODIC TENANCY** (ENGLAND)
C		**RESTRICTED CONTRACT LETTING** (ENGLAND)
D		**PROTECTED OR STATUTORY TENANCY** (ENGLAND)
E		**ASSURED OR SHORT ASSURED TENANCY** (SCOTLAND)
F		**PRIVATE TENANCY** (NORTHERN IRELAND)
G		**LODGER** (ENGLAND, WALES, SCOTLAND OR NORTHERN IRELAND)

If you are unsure which type of letting applies to your property, seek legal advice.

FOR TENANTS IN ENGLAND

INFORMATION FOR TENANT

IMPORTANT: please read this and the notices and information on pages 4 to 7.

As a tenant, if the rent for the premises you occupy as your residence is payable weekly, the landlord must provide you with a rent book or similar document. If you have an Assured Tenancy, including an Assured Periodic Tenancy, or a Restricted Contract Letting, or a Protected or Statutory Tenancy (see paragraphs A9, B11 and C11 on pages 5, 6 and 7), the rent book or similar document must contain the notices and information which are appropriate to your type of tenancy on pages 4 to 7, properly filled in.

The landlord must complete a table (see below), stating the current rent and charge for services/improvements (if any), with the total figure in the end column. If these figures change, the landlord should insert the new figures, together with the date they are effective from.

The premises are let weekly at the rent shown, which is payable on ____________ each week in advance/arrears* and which includes the sums (if any) stated in respect of service, etc.

	WEEKLY PAYMENTS		
EFFECTIVE FROM	CHARGES FOR SERVICES, IMPROVEMENTS, ETC	RENT (SEE DETAILS ON PAGES 6-8)	TOTAL PAYABLE
	(£)	(£)	(£)
DATE			
DATE			
DATE			
DATE			
DATE			
DATE			
DATE			
DATE			

** Delete as appropriate*

Note – this section is for both Assured and Assured Periodic tenants. Therefore any mention of assured tenancies should not be taken as giving notice that the tenancy is an assured tenancy.

Notices and information which apply to all types of letting:

THE HOUSING ACT 1985

Summary of Part X of the Housing Act 1985.

CAUSING OR PERMITTING OVERCROWDING

1. An occupier who causes or permits his dwelling to be overcrowded is liable to prosecution for an offence under the Housing Act 1985, and, if convicted, to a fine of up to level 2 on the standard scale, and a further fine of up to one-tenth of that level in respect of every day on which the offence continues after conviction. Any part of a house which is occupied by a separate household is a 'dwelling'.
2. A dwelling is overcrowded if the number of persons sleeping in it is more than the 'permitted number', or is such that two or more of those persons, being ten years old or over, of opposite sexes (not being persons living together as husband and wife), must sleep in the same room.
3. The 'permitted number' for the dwelling to which this Rent Book relates is ____________ persons. In counting the number of persons each child under ten counts as half a person, and a child of less than a year is not counted at all.

   The name and address of the local environmental health officer is:

   ____

   ____

   Tel: ______________________________

   The name and address of the landlord or other person responsible for repairs is:

   ____

   ____

   Tel: ______________________________

RENT BOOK (FORMS OF NOTICE) REGULATIONS 1982 AS AMENDED

* *These entries must be kept up to date* ** *Delete as appropriate*

1. Address of premises

   ____

   ____

   ____

2. Name and address of landlord*

   ____

   ____

3. Name and address of agent (if any)*

____

____

4. The rent payable [including council tax (cross out if council tax is not payable to the landlord)] [and including rates (cross out if rates are not payable to the landlord)] is £ __________ per week. *

5. Details of accommodation (if any) which the occupier has the right to share with other persons

____

____

6. The other terms and conditions of the tenancy are [as set out in your tenancy agreement dated / as set out below] **

____

____

7. You may be entitled to get help to pay your rent through the Housing Benefit scheme or through Universal Credit. Apply to your local council or to the Department for Work and Pensions for details. The gov.uk website provides further advice: www.gov.uk.

8. If you are in any doubt about your legal rights or obligations, particularly if your landlord has asked you to leave, you should go to a Citizens Advice Bureau, housing aid centre, law centre, or solicitor. Help with all or part of the cost of legal advice from a solicitor may be available under the Legal Aid Scheme.

NB These numbered paragraphs continue in each of the three sections set out below, only one of which will apply to you.

Notices and information which apply to different types of letting:

(Your landlord should delete the sections which do not apply to you.)

A. ASSURED TENANCY OR ASSURED PERIODIC TENANCY OR ASSURED AGRICULTURAL OCCUPANCY

Note: Most tenancies created after 15th January 1989 will be Assured or Assured Periodic Tenancies.

9. If you have an assured tenancy or an Assured Agricultural Occupancy you have certain rights under the Housing Act 1988. These include the right not to be evicted from your home unless your landlord gets a possession order from the courts. Unless the property is let under an Assured Periodic Tenancy, the courts can only grant an order on a limited number of grounds. Further details regarding assured tenancies are set out in the Department of the Environment, Transport and the Regions and Welsh Office booklet 'Assured Tenancies' no. 19 in the series of housing booklets. These booklets are available from rent officers, council offices and housing aid centres, some of which also give advice.

10. It is a criminal offence for your landlord to evict you without an order from the court or to harass you or interfere with your possessions or use of facilities in order to force you to leave. Nothing in this Rent Book constitutes a notice under paragraph 1 of Schedule 2A of the Housing Act 1988 (as amended) that your tenancy is to be an Assured Tenancy.

B. RESTRICTED CONTRACT LETTINGS

Note: Under the Housing Act 1988 (section 36) no new restricted contracts can be created. However the Act did not abolish restricted contract lettings that existed at the time it came into force. If a rent is registered by the First-tier Tribunal, paragraph 9 and, where it applies, paragraph 10 must be filled in, otherwise they should be crossed out.

9. The registered rent (which excludes rates, but includes any council tax payable to the landlord) is £ ______________ per week, registered on ______________(date).*

10. In addition to the registered rent, £ ____________ per week is payable to cover rates paid by the landlord or a superior landlord.*

11. Restricted contracts are usually lettings by landlords who live in the same house. There are rules about your rights to stay in the accommodation and the rent you pay for restricted contracts. Details of these rules are set out in the Department of the Environment, Transport and the Regions and Welsh Office booklets 'Letting Rooms in Your Home' and 'Notice That You Must Leave', nos. 22 and 24 in the series of housing booklets. These booklets are obtainable free from rent officers, council offices and housing aid centres, some of which also give advice.

12. If your letting began on or after 28th November 1980, you cannot be evicted unless the landlord gets a possession order from the courts. The rules for lettings which began before 28th November 1980 are different. You may have the right to apply to the First-tier Tribunal to postpone any notice to quit and the landlord often also needs a court order. Whether your letting began before or after 28th November 1980, either you or the landlord can apply to the same tribunal to fix a reasonable rent. It is unwise to apply without first getting advice.

13. It is a criminal offence for your landlord to harass you or interfere with your possessions or use of facilities in order to force you to leave.

C. PROTECTED OR STATUTORY TENANCIES

Note: Under the Housing Act 1988 (section 34) in general no new protected or statutory tenancies can be created. However the Act did not abolish restricted protected or statutory tenancies that existed at the time it came into force.

If a fair rent is registered paragraph 9 and, where it applies, paragraph 10 must be filled in, otherwise they should be crossed out.

9. The registered rent (which excludes rates, but includes any council tax payable to the landlord) is £ ______________ per week, effective from____________________ (date).*

If the rent is registered as variable (because it includes service charges which vary), this should be indicated by placing a tick in the box. ☐

10. In addition to the registered rent, £ __________ per week is payable to cover rates paid by the landlord or a superior landlord.*

11. You are protected by the Rent Act 1977 and known as a 'regulated tenant'. The Rent Act contains important rules concerning the amount of rent you have to pay and your rights to stay in your home. Details of these rules are set out in the Department of the Environment, Transport and the Regions and Welsh Office booklets 'Regulated Tenancies' and 'Notice That You Must Leave', nos. 25 and 22. These booklets are available from rent officers, council offices, and housing aid centres, some of which also give advice.

12. Either you or your landlord may apply to the rent officer for a fair rent to be registered. It is wise to get advice before doing so. Whether or not your rent is registered by the rent officer there are rules about how and when it can be increased. You cannot be evicted from your home unless your landlord gets a possession order from the courts, and the courts can grant an order only in special circumstances.

13. If you have a protected shorthold tenancy or your tenancy was formerly a controlled one, special rules apply.

14. It is a criminal offence for your landlord to evict you without an order from the court or to harass you or interfere with your possessions or use of facilities in order to force you to leave.

FOR LODGERS IN ENGLAND & WALES
Notice and information which apply to LODGERS

Nothing in this document constitutes any form of creation of a tenancy or other similar right. Any payments made by you or on your behalf will not be accepted as rent but only as a fee for occupancy.

There is no legal obligation to provide lodgers with a payment book; but keeping one is good practice.

FOR TENANTS IN SCOTLAND

INFORMATION FOR TENANT

IMPORTANT: please read this and the notices and information on pages 9-11.

As a tenant, if the rent for the premises you occupy as your residence is payable weekly, the landlord must provide you with a rent book or similar document. If you have an Assured Tenancy, including a Short Assured Tenancy, the rent book or similar document must contain the notices and information which are appropriate to your type of tenancy on pages 9 to 11, properly filled in.

The landlord must complete a table (see below), stating the current rent and charge for services/improvements (if any), with the total figure in the end column. If these figures change, the landlord should insert the new figures, together with the date they are effective from.

The premises are let weekly at the rent shown, which is payable on ____________ each week in advance/arrears* and which includes the sums (if any) stated in respect of service, etc.

	WEEKLY PAYMENTS		
EFFECTIVE FROM	**CHARGES FOR SERVICES, IMPROVEMENTS, ETC**	**RENT (SEE DETAILS ON PAGES 9)**	**TOTAL PAYABLE**
	(£)	**(£)**	**(£)**
DATE			
DATE			
DATE			
DATE			
DATE			
DATE			
DATE			
DATE			

** Delete as appropriate*

FORM OF RENT BOOK

Form under Section 79(1) of the Rent (Scotland) Act 1984

INFORMATION FOR TENANTS

NOTE: You occupy this dwelling-house under a contract to which Part VII of the Rent (Scotland) Act 1984 applies. This affects the rent which your landlord may lawfully recover and confers a degree of security of tenure. Your landlord must keep the entries up to date.

1. Address of the dwelling-house and description of the premises to which the contract relates

____

____

2. Name, address and telephone number of landlord and of the landlord's agent (if any)

____

____

RENT LAWFULLY RECOVERABLE

3. a) If no rent is registered

(i) The rent payable as from __________ is £ _____ per week.

(ii) If furniture or services are provided the amount (if any) which is apportioned to them under the contract is:

Furniture £ _________ Services £ _________

b) If a reasonable rent has been registered following determination by the rent officer:

a) *A rent of £ _________ per week for the dwelling-house comprised in the contract was approved by the rent officer on _________.

b) *The rent for the dwelling-house comprised in the contract was *reduced/increased* by the rent officer to £ _________ on _________.

**Delete if inapplicable*

ALTERATIONS IN RENT

4. a) Either you or the landlord may refer the contract to the rent officer to fix a reasonable rent. On such a reference, the rent officer may approve the rent payable under the contract or may reduce or increase the rent to such sum as the rent officer considers reasonable or may, if the rent officer thinks fit in all the circumstances dismiss the reference. Any approval, reduction or increase may be limited to the rent payable in respect of a particular period.

b) The rent determined by the rent officer is registered and it then becomes a criminal offence for any person to require or receive, on account of rent for that dwelling under any contract, more than the registered rent. Any overpayment of rent may be recovered by you.

c) Once a rent has been registered, then for three years after the rent was last considered by the rent officer no new application for the registration of a different rent can be made, except by you and the landlord acting together, or where there has been a change in the circumstances taken into account when the rent was last considered – for example, a change in the terms of the tenancy or in the furniture supplied, or in the condition of the dwelling-house.

d) If you agree to a change in rent or any other terms of the contract without reference to the rent officer you will no longer have a Part VII contract.

SECURITY OF TENURE

5. a) The landlord can recover possession of a dwelling-house subject to a Part VII contract only by obtaining an order for possession from the First-tier Tribunal for Scotland (the Tribunal). This means that if the landlord serves a notice to quit on you, you do not have to leave by the date stated in the notice. If you feel you cannot leave at that time, before you can be evicted the landlord must first get an order for possession from the Tribunal.

b) A tenancy cannot be terminated until a valid notice is served. To be valid a notice to quit must be in proper form and in writing and give at least four weeks' notice.

c) When the notice to quit takes effect the landlord is entitled, if you do not leave voluntarily, to obtain an order for possession of the dwelling-house from the Tribunal. The landlord cannot evict you from the dwelling without such an order from the Tribunal and it is a criminal offence for him or her or for anyone to try to make you leave by using force, by threatening you or your family, by withdrawing services or by interfering with your home or your possessions. If anyone does this, you should contact the police immediately.

HOUSING BENEFIT

6. If you have difficulty in paying your the rent, should apply to your local authority for Housing Benefit. You may obtain further information on Housing Benefit from your local authority Offices or Citizens' Advice Bureau.

FOR LODGERS IN SCOTLAND

Notice and information which apply to LODGERS

Nothing in this document constitutes any form of creation of a tenancy or other right to heritable property. Any payments made by you or on your behalf will not be accepted as rent but only as a fee for occupancy.

There is no legal obligation to provide lodgers with a payment book; but keeping one is good practice.

FOR TENANTS IN NORTHERN IRELAND

Information for tenant

Under the Private Tenancies (Northern Ireland) Order 2006 all tenants are required to be provided with a rent book within 28 days after the start date of the tenancy, irrespective of how the rent is paid.

It is your responsibility to keep this rent book safe and to provide it to your landlord, on reasonable request, for it to be kept up to date.

The landlord must complete all the information below and must make arrangements with you to keep the rent book up to date.

LANDLORD REGISTRATION NUMBER

___

The Rent Book Regulations (Northern Ireland) 2007

** These entries must be kept up to date ** Delete as appropriate*

ADDRESS OF PREMISES

___

___

___

NAME OF TENANT(S)

___

___

___

NAME, ADDRESS, AND TELEPHONE NUMBER OF LANDLORD*

___

___

___

NAME, ADDRESS, AND TELEPHONE NUMBER OF AGENT (IF ANY)*

___

___

___

The rent payable is £ _________* per week/4 weeks/month/ 6 months/ year/other**

- The capital value of the premises is £ ___________
- The rates payable for the premises are £ ____________
- The amount of £ _________ in respect of the rates is included in/ payable in addition to** the rent for the period of _______________
- The tenant is also required to pay to the landlord the sum of £_______ in respect of _______________________________
- The tenancy begins on _________________________ 20 ____

FOR LODGERS IN NORTHERN IRELAND

Notice and information which apply to LODGERS

Nothing in this document constitutes any form of creation of a tenancy or other similar right. Any payments made by you or on your behalf will not be accepted as rent but only as a fee for occupancy.

There is no legal obligation to provide lodgers with a payment book; but keeping one is good practice.

DATE DUE	RENT DUE £		DATE RECEIVED

CASH RECEIVED	ARREARS £	BY WHOM RECEIVED

DATE DUE	RENT DUE £	DATE RECEIVED

CASH RECEIVED	ARREARS £	BY WHOM RECEIVED

LAWPACK®

A rent book or similar document is required by law in those tenancy situations where rent is paid on a weekly basis.

This Lawpack Rent Book & Guidance provides information and instructions for collecting and recording the payment of rent in these commonly occurring types of letting situation:

- **Assured and Assured Periodic Tenancies, Restricted Contract Lettings and Protected or Statutory Tenancies in England**
- **Assured and Short Assured Tenancies in Scotland**
- **Private Tenancies in Northern Ireland**
- **Lodgers in England & Wales, Scotland, and Northern Ireland**

It includes all the notices and information for tenants that are required by law, and pages for recording 78 weeks' (18 months') rent.

ISBN 978 1 913714 55 0

9 781913 714550 >

LAWYER APPROVED

This Rent Book has been approved by solicitors under the laws of England, Northern Ireland, and Scotland.

0P6